CHINESE
HOROSCOPES
FOR
LOVERS

The
Rat

LORI REID

illustrated by
PAUL COLLICUTT

ELEMENT BOOKS

Shaftesbury, Dorset • Rockport, Massachusetts • Brisbane, Queensland

© Lori Reid 1996

First published in Great Britain in 1995 by

ELEMENT BOOKS LIMITED

Shaftesbury, Dorset SP7 8BP

Published in the USA in 1996 by

ELEMENT BOOKS, INC.

PO Box 830, Rockport, MA 01966

Published in Australia in 1996 by

ELEMENT BOOKS LIMITED

for JACARANDA WILEY LIMITED

33 Park Road, Milton, Brisbane 4064

Designed and created by

THE BRIDGEWATER BOOK COMPANY

Art directed by *Peter Bridgewater*

Designed by *Angela Neal*

Picture research by *Vanessa Fletcher*

Edited by *Gillian Delaforce*

Printed and bound in Great Britain by
BPC Paulton Books Ltd

British Library Cataloguing in Publication data available

Library of Congress Cataloging in Publication data available

ISBN 1-85230-759-5

Contents

THE
RAT

8

*Why are
some people
lucky in
love and
others not?*

Chinese Astrology

SOME PEOPLE fall in love and, as the fairy tales go, live happily ever after. Others fall in love – again and again, make the same mistakes every time and never form a lasting relationship. Most of us come between these two extremes,

and some people form remarkably successful unions while others make spectacular disasters of their personal lives. Why are some people lucky in love while others have the odds stacked against them?

ANIMAL NAMES
According to the philosophy of the Far East, luck has very little to do with it. The answer, the philosophers say, lies with 'the Animal that hides in our hearts'. This Animal, of which there are 12, forms part of the complex art of Chinese Astrology. Each year of a 12-year cycle is attributed an Animal sign, whose characteristics are said to influence worldly events as well as the personality and fate of each living thing that comes under its dominion. The 12 Animals run in sequence, beginning with the Rat and followed by the Ox, Tiger, Rabbit, Dragon, Snake, Horse, Sheep, Monkey, Rooster, Dog and last, but not least, the Pig. Being born in the Year of the Ox, for example, is simply a way of describing what you're like, physically and psychologically. And this is quite different from someone who, for instance, is born in the Year of the Snake.

鼠

9

*Firing Crackers at the
New Year festival*
CHINESE PAINTING

*The 12
Animals
of Chinese
Astrology*

RELATIONSHIPS

These Animal names are merely the tip of the ice-berg,
considering the complexity of the whole subject. Yet such
are the richness and wisdom of Chinese Astrology that understanding
the principles behind the year in which you were born will give you
powerful insights into your own personality. The system is very
specific about which Animals are compatible and which are
antagonistic and this tells us whether our relationships will be
successful. Marriages are made in heaven, so the saying goes. The
heavens, according to Chinese beliefs, can point the way. The rest is
up to us.

Year Chart and Birth Dates

UNLIKE THE WESTERN CALENDAR, which is based on the Sun, the Oriental year is based on the movement of the Moon, which means that New Year's Day does not fall on a fixed date. This Year Chart, taken from the Chinese Perpetual Calendar, lists the dates on which each year begins and ends together with its Animal ruler for the year. In addition, the Chinese believe that the tangible world is composed of 5 elements, each slightly adapting the characteristics of the Animal signs. These elemental influences are also given here. Finally, the aspect, that is, whether the year is characteristically Yin (-) or Yang (+), is also listed.

The Western calendar is based on the Sun; the Oriental on the Moon.

YIN AND YANG

Yin and Yang are the terms given to the dynamic complementary forces that keep the universe in balance and which are the central principles behind life. Yin is all that is considered negative, passive, feminine, night, the Moon, while Yang is considered positive, active, masculine, day, the Sun.

鼠

11

Year	From – To		Animal sign	Element	Aspect	
1900	31 Jan 1900 – 18 Feb 1901		Rat	Metal	+	Yang
1901	19 Feb 1901 – 7 Feb 1902		Ox	Metal	–	Yin
1902	8 Feb 1902 – 28 Jan 1903		Tiger	Water	+	Yang
1903	29 Jan 1903 – 15 Feb 1904		Rabbit	Water	–	Yin
1904	16 Feb 1904 – 3 Feb 1905		Dragon	Wood	+	Yang
1905	4 Feb 1905 – 24 Jan 1906		Snake	Wood	–	Yin
1906	25 Jan 1906 – 12 Feb 1907		Horse	Fire	+	Yang
1907	13 Feb 1907 – 1 Feb 1908		Sheep	Fire	–	Yin
1908	2 Feb 1908 – 21 Jan 1909		Monkey	Earth	+	Yang
1909	22 Jan 1909 – 9 Feb 1910		Rooster	Earth	–	Yin
1910	10 Feb 1910 – 29 Jan 1911		Dog	Metal	+	Yang
1911	30 Jan 1911 – 17 Feb 1912		Pig	Metal	–	Yin
1912	18 Feb 1912 – 5 Feb 1913		Rat	Water	+	Yang
1913	6 Feb 1913 – 25 Jan 1914		Ox	Water	–	Yin
1914	26 Jan 1914 – 13 Feb 1915		Tiger	Wood	+	Yang
1915	14 Feb 1915 – 2 Feb 1916		Rabbit	Wood	–	Yin
1916	3 Feb 1916 – 22 Jan 1917		Dragon	Fire	+	Yang
1917	23 Jan 1917 – 10 Feb 1918		Snake	Fire	–	Yin
1918	11 Feb 1918 – 31 Jun 1919		Horse	Earth	+	Yang
1919	1 Feb 1919 – 19 Feb 1920		Sheep	Earth	–	Yin
1920	20 Feb 1920 – 7 Feb 1921		Monkey	Metal	+	Yang
1921	8 Feb 1921 – 27 Jan 1922		Rooster	Metal	–	Yin
1922	28 Jan 1922 – 15 Feb 1923		Dog	Water	+	Yang
1923	16 Feb 1923 – 4 Feb 1924		Pig	Water	–	Yin
1924	5 Feb 1924 – 24 Jan 1925		Rat	Wood	+	Yang
1925	25 Jan 1925 – 12 Feb 1926		Ox	Wood	–	Yin
1926	13 Feb 1926 – 1 Feb 1927		Tiger	Fire	+	Yang
1927	2 Feb 1927 – 22 Jan 1928		Rabbit	Fire	–	Yin
1928	23 Jan 1928 – 9 Feb 1929		Dragon	Earth	+	Yang
1929	10 Feb 1929 – 29 Jan 1930		Snake	Earth	–	Yin
1930	30 Jan 1930 – 16 Feb 1931		Horse	Metal	+	Yang
1931	17 Feb 1931 – 5 Feb 1932		Sheep	Metal	–	Yin
1932	6 Feb 1932 – 25 Jan 1933		Monkey	Water	+	Yang
1933	26 Jan 1933 – 13 Feb 1934		Rooster	Water	–	Yin
1934	14 Feb 1934 – 3 Feb 1935		Dog	Wood	+	Yang
1935	4 Feb 1935 – 23 Jan 1936		Pig	Wood	–	Yin

鼠

12

Year	From – To	Animal sign	Element	Aspect	
1936	24 Jan 1936 – 10 Feb 1937	Rat	Fire	+	Yang
1937	11 Feb 1937 – 30 Jan 1938	Ox	Fire	–	Yin
1938	31 Jan 1938 – 18 Feb 1939	Tiger	Earth	+	Yang
1939	19 Feb 1939 – 7 Feb 1940	Rabbit	Earth	–	Yin
1940	8 Feb 1940 – 26 Jan 1941	Dragon	Metal	+	Yang
1941	27 Jan 1941 – 14 Feb 1942	Snake	Metal	–	Yin
1942	15 Feb 1942 – 4 Feb 1943	Horse	Water	+	Yang
1943	5 Feb 1943 – 24 Jan 1944	Sheep	Water	–	Yin
1944	25 Jan 1944 – 12 Feb 1945	Monkey	Wood	+	Yang
1945	13 Feb 1945 – 1 Feb 1946	Rooster	Wood	–	Yin
1946	2 Feb 1946 – 21 Jan 1947	Dog	Fire	+	Yang
1947	22 Jan 1947 – 9 Feb 1948	Pig	Fire	–	Yin
1948	10 Feb 1948 – 28 Jan 1949	Rat	Earth	+	Yang
1949	29 Jan 1949 – 16 Feb 1950	Ox	Earth	–	Yin
1950	17 Feb 1950 –5 Feb 1951	Tiger	Metal	+	Yang
1951	6 Feb 1951 – 26 Jan 1952	Rabbit	Metal	–	Yin
1952	27 Jan 1952 – 13 Feb 1953	Dragon	Water	+	Yang
1953	14 Feb 1953 – 2 Feb 1954	Snake	Water	–	Yin
1954	3 Feb 1954 – 23 Jan 1955	Horse	Wood	+	Yang
1955	24 Jan 1955 – 11 Feb 1956	Sheep	Wood	–	Yin
1956	12 Feb 1956 – 30 Jan 1957	Monkey	Fire	+	Yang
1957	31 Jan 1957 – 17 Feb 1958	Rooster	Fire	–	Yin
1958	18 Feb 1958 – 7 Feb 1959	Dog	Earth	+	Yang
1959	8 Feb 1959 – 27 Jan 1960	Pig	Earth	–	Yin
1960	28 Jan 1960 – 14 Feb 1961	Rat	Metal	+	Yang
1961	15 Feb 1961 – 4 Feb 1962	Ox	Metal	–	Yin
1962	5 Feb 1962 – 24 Jan 1963	Tiger	Water	+	Yang
1963	25 Jan 1963 – 12 Feb 1964	Rabbit	Water	–	Yin
1964	13 Feb 1964 – 1 Feb 1965	Dragon	Wood	+	Yang
1965	2 Feb 1965 – 20 Jan 1966	Snake	Wood	–	Yin
1966	21 Jan 1966 – 8 Feb 1967	Horse	Fire	+	Yang
1967	9 Feb 1967 – 29 Jan 1968	Sheep	Fire	–	Yin
1968	30 Jan 1968 – 16 Feb 1969	Monkey	Earth	+	Yang
1969	17 Feb 1969 – 5 Feb 1970	Rooster	Earth	–	Yin
1970	6 Feb 1970 – 26 Jan 1971	Dog	Metal	+	Yang
1971	27 Jan 1971 – 15 Jan 1972	Pig	Metal	–	Yin

鼠

13

Year	From – To		Animal sign	Element	Aspect	
1972	16 Jan 1972 – 2 Feb 1973		Rat	Water	+	Yang
1973	3 Feb 1973 – 22 Jan 1974		Ox	Water	–	Yin
1974	23 Jan 1974 – 10 Feb 1975		Tiger	Wood	+	Yang
1975	11 Feb 1975 – 30 Jan 1976		Rabbit	Wood	–	Yin
1976	31 Jan 1976 – 17 Feb 1977		Dragon	Fire	+	Yang
1977	18 Feb 1977 – 6 Feb 1978		Snake	Fire	–	Yin
1978	7 Feb 1978 – 27 Jan 1979		Horse	Earth	+	Yang
1979	28 Jan 1979 – 15 Feb 1980		Sheep	Earth	–	Yin
1980	16 Feb 1980 – 4 Feb 1981		Monkey	Metal	+	Yang
1981	5 Feb 1981 – 24 Jan 1982		Rooster	Metal	–	Yin
1982	25 Jan 1982 – 12 Feb 1983		Dog	Water	+	Yang
1983	13 Feb 1983 – 1 Feb 1984		Pig	Water	–	Yin
1984	2 Feb 1984 – 19 Feb 1985		Rat	Wood	+	Yang
1985	20 Feb 1985 – 8 Feb 1986		Ox	Wood	–	Yin
1986	9 Feb 1986 – 28 Jan 1987		Tiger	Fire	+	Yang
1987	29 Jan 1987 – 16 Feb 1988		Rabbit	Fire	–	Yin
1988	17 Feb 1988 – 5 Feb 1989		Dragon	Earth	+	Yang
1989	6 Feb 1989 – 26 Jan 1990		Snake	Earth	–	Yin
1990	27 Jan 1990 – 14 Feb 1991		Horse	Metal	+	Yang
1991	15 Feb 1991 – 3 Feb 1992		Sheep	Metal	–	Yin
1992	4 Feb 1992 – 22 Jan 1993		Monkey	Water	+	Yang
1993	23 Jan 1993 – 9 Feb 1994		Rooster	Water	–	Yin
1994	10 Feb 1994 – 30 Jan 1995		Dog	Wood	+	Yang
1995	31 Jan 1995 – 18 Feb 1996		Pig	Wood	–	Yin
1996	19 Feb 1996 – 7 Feb 1997		Rat	Fire	+	Yang
1997	8 Feb 1997 – 27 Jan 1998		Ox	Fire	–	Yin
1998	28 Jan 1998 – 15 Feb 1999		Tiger	Earth	+	Yang
1999	16 Feb 1999 – 4 Feb 2000		Rabbit	Earth	–	Yin
2000	5 Feb 2000 – 23 Jan 2001		Dragon	Metal	+	Yang
2001	24 Jan 2001 – 11 Feb 2002		Snake	Metal	–	Yin
2002	12 Feb 2002 – 31 Jan 2003		Horse	Water	+	Yang
2003	1 Feb 2003 – 21 Jan 2004		Sheep	Water	–	Yin
2004	22 Jan 2004 – 8 Feb 2005		Monkey	Wood	+	Yang
2005	9 Feb 2005 – 28 Jan 2006		Rooster	Wood	–	Yin
2006	29 Jan 2006 – 17 Feb 2007		Dog	Fire	+	Yang
2007	18 Feb 2007 – 6 Feb 2008		Pig	Fire	–	Yin

14

Introducing the Animals

THE RAT ♥ ♥ ♥ DRAGON, MONKEY ✖ HORSE

Outwardly cool, Rats are passionate lovers with depths of feeling that others don't often recognize. Rats are very self-controlled.

THE OX ♥ ♥ ♥ SNAKE, ROOSTER ✖ SHEEP

Not necessarily the most romantic of the signs, Ox people make steadfast lovers as well as faithful, affectionate partners.

THE TIGER ♥ ♥ ♥ HORSE, DOG ✖ MONKEY

Passionate and sensual, Tigers are exciting lovers. Flirty when young, once committed they make stable partners and keep their sexual allure.

THE RABBIT ♥ ♥ ♥ SHEEP, PIG ✖ ROOSTER

Gentle, emotional and sentimental, Rabbits make sensitive lovers. They are shrewd and seek a partner who offers security.

THE DRAGON ♥ ♥ ♥ RAT, MONKEY ✖ DOG

Dragon folk get as much stimulation from mind-touch as they do through sex. A partner on the same wave-length is essential.

THE SNAKE ♥ ♥ ♥ OX, ROOSTER ✖ PIG

Deeply passionate, strongly sexed but not aggressive, snakes are attracted to elegant, refined partners. But they are deeply jealous and possessive.

♥ ♥ ♥ *COMPATIBLE*   ✖ *INCOMPATIBLE*

| THE HORSE | ♥ ♥ ♥ TIGER, DOG | ✖ RAT |

For horse-born folk love is blind. In losing their hearts, they lose their heads and make several mistakes before finding the right partner.

鼠

15

| THE SHEEP | ♥ ♥ ♥ RABBIT, PIG | ✖ OX |

Sheep-born people are made for marriage. Domesticated home-lovers, they find emotional satisfaction with a partner who provides security.

| THE MONKEY | ♥ ♥ ♥ DRAGON, RAT | ✖ TIGER |

Clever and witty, Monkeys need partners who will keep them stimulated. Forget the 9 to 5 routine, these people need *pizzazz*.

| THE ROOSTER | ♥ ♥ ♥ OX, SNAKE | ✖ RABBIT |

The Rooster's stylish good looks guarantee they will attract many suitors. They are level-headed and approach relationships coolly.

| THE DOG | ♥ ♥ ♥ TIGER, HORSE | ✖ DRAGON |

A loving, stable relationship is an essential component in the lives of Dogs. Once they have found their mate, they remain faithful for life.

| THE PIG | ♥ ♥ ♥ RABBIT, SHEEP | ✖ SNAKE |

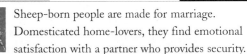

These are sensual hedonists who enjoy lingering love-making between satin sheets. Caviar and champagne go down very nicely too.

16

The Rat Personality

YEARS OF THE RAT

1900 ★ 1912 ★ 1924 ★ 1936 ★ 1948 ★ 1960
1972 ★ 1984 ★ 1996 ★ 2008

IN CHINA, the Rat is respected, unlike in the West where it is despised. Being born a Rat is nothing to be ashamed of. You should be proud to be governed by this esteemed influence. Rats are clever creatures. They know instinctively where to find the fat sacks of grain and flour upon which to feast in times of plenty. When corn is scarce, they know where to forage for rich pickings. Such resourcefulness ensures that these creatures are natural survivors.

RAT FACTS

First in order ★ *Chinese name – SHU* ★ *Sign of charm*
★ *Hour – 11PM–12.59AM* ★ *Month - December* ★
★ *Western counterpart – Sagittarius* ★

CHARACTERISTICS

♥ *Charisma* ♥ *Affability* ♥ *Intelligence* ♥ *Sociability*
♥ *Quickwittedness* ♥ *Popularity*

✖ *Exploitation* ✖ *Deviousness* ✖ *Calculation* ✖ *Secretiveness*
✖ *Greed* ✖ *Acquisitiveness*

Night Battle
KAO CHIH-MIN
PAINTING

THE SIGN OF THE RAT

Being born under the sign of the Rat means that you are blessed with the listed talents and characteristics. With your active brain you need a lot of stimulation, but sometimes you're tempted to take on too much and find that you can't fulfil all your commitments. That you're clever is undeniable; you have one of the best intellects going. To your curiosity and considerable imagination is added a penetrative insight that makes you sharp as a new pin.

THE FIRST SIGN

Yours is the first sign in the cycle and this imbues you with leadership qualities; you like to be first. Responsibility sits well on you and you are a strong presence that others respect. Your Rat nature means that power and money are your driving forces.

Power and money are driving forces for the Rat.

18

Your Hour of Birth

WHILE YOUR YEAR OF BIRTH describes your fundamental character, the Animal governing the actual hour in which you were born describes your outer temperament, how people see you or the picture you present to the outside world. Note that each Animal rules over two consecutive hours. Also note that these are GMT standard times and that adjustments need to be made if you were born during Summer or daylight saving time.

11PM – 12.59AM ★ RAT
Pleasant, sociable, easy to get on with. An active, confident, busy person – and a bit of a busybody to boot.

1AM – 2.59AM ★ OX
Level-headed and down-to-earth, you come across as knowledgeable and reliable – sometimes, though, a bit biased.

3AM – 4.59AM ★ TIGER
Enthusiastic and self-assured, people see you as a strong and positive personality – at times a little over-exuberant.

5AM – 6.59AM ★ RABBIT
You're sensitive and shy and don't project your real self to the world. You feel you have to put on an act to please others.

7AM – 8.59AM ★ DRAGON
Independent and interesting, you present a picture of someone who is quite out of the ordinary.

9AM – 10.59AM ★ SNAKE
You can be a bit difficult to fathom and, because you appear so controlled, people either take to you instantly, or not at all.

11AM – 12.59PM ★ HORSE

 Open, cheerful and happy-go-lucky is the picture you always put across to others. You're an extrovert and it generally shows.

1PM – 2.59PM ★ SHEEP

Your unassuming nature won't allow you to foist yourself upon others so people see you as quiet and retiring – but eminently sensible, though.

3PM – 4.59PM ★ MONKEY

Lively and talkative, that twinkle in your eye will guarantee you make friends wherever you go.

5PM – 6.59PM ★ ROOSTER

 There's something rather stylish in your approach that gives people an impression of elegance and glamour. But you don't suffer fools gladly.

7PM – 8.59PM ★ DOG

Some people see you as steady and reliable, others as quiet and graceful and others still as dull and unimaginative. It all depends who you're with at the time.

9PM – 10.59PM ★ PIG

Your laid-back manner conceals a depth of interest and intelligence that doesn't always come through at first glance.

Your hour of birth describes your outer temperament.

鼠

20

If you're true to your sign, you'll be driven by your senses and will enjoy indulging in physical pleasures, so the whole business of sex is terrifically thrilling for you. In love you're highly sensual and your love-making is likely to be hot and steamy, but, though you're intense, you're also a generous lover, making sure your partner receives as much pleasure as you do.

Rats are romantic and fall in love easily.

The Rat Lover

THERE ARE NO two ways about it, Rats are attractive people with bags of personal magnetism that draws members of the opposite sex like bees around a honey-pot. Surely, you can't have failed to notice all those admiring glances? If, as the Chinese say, there are very few poor Rats, then there must be even fewer who don't fairly drip with sex-appeal – certainly so in their younger days. You're romantic and fall in love easily. Perhaps this is because single Rats are lonely creatures and are much happier when they have a partner by their sides.

RAT CHARM

As a Rat, one of your biggest assets is your charm. You can melt a person's heart with a smile. Add that to your flirtatious nature and you can see how easily you make conquests. And, as Rats are made for the night life, you'll have plenty of opportunities to meet up with potential mates and have the odd fling.

鼠

21

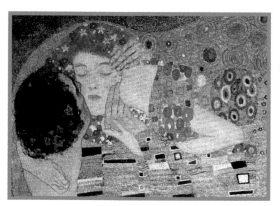

The Kiss
GUSTAV KLIMT 1862-1918

EMOTIONAL TIES

A quirk amongst some of you Rat lovers is that you find it difficult to completely sever emotional ties between you and your former lovers. Do beware, as this can prove a source of friction with a new lover and may jeopardize the development of the new relationship. But when you do eventually meet and settle down with Mr or Ms Right, love will be stimulating and you will find a deep fulfilment in the warm intimacy of the relationship.

Rats are also charming and flirtatious.

22

In Your Element

ALTHOUGH YOUR SIGN recurs every 12 years, each generation is slightly modified by one of 5 elements. If you were born under the Metal influence your character, emotions and behaviour would show significant variations from an individual born under one of the other elements. Check the Year Chart for your ruling element and discover what effects it has upon you.

THE METAL RAT ★ 1900 AND 1960

Of all the elemental Rats, you're the strongest and most purposeful. Stubborn and single-minded, you like being in charge. In partnerships you can be unyielding. Meeting your partner half-way would make relationships considerably smoother.

THE WATER RAT ★ 1912 AND 1972

Being governed by the Water element means you have the knack of influencing people. Though you possess strong intellectual powers, you're also understanding and innately practical – talents that you apply sympathetically to your everyday life. Amenable and flexible, you are generally liked and respected by all.

鼠

23

THE WOOD RAT ★ 1924 AND 1984

Despite your façade of self-assurance, you're probably the least confident of all the elemental Rats. But you wouldn't dream of showing this to all and sundry – only those close to you would ever suspect your self-doubts. Anxious about failure, you function best with the protective security of family around you. Friendly and sensitive, you're generally well-loved.

THE FIRE RAT ★ 1936 AND 1996

Impatient and impulsive, routine is definitely not for you, so you're likely to change jobs and addresses more than most. But your enthusiasm for life is quite infectious. In comparison to other Rats, you're likely to be the most generous, independent and dynamic – but the least self-disciplined of all.

THE EARTH RAT ★ 1948 AND 2008

Conservative, you're a solid achiever who likes to put down roots early on and then work towards a secure future for yourself and your family. Although not the most generous of the elemental groups, you have great integrity. A steady accumulation of wealth through your life gives you peace of mind.

鼠

24

*Rencontre
du Soir
(detail)*
THEOPHILE-
ALEXANDRE
STEINLEN
1859–1923

Partners in Love

THE CHINESE are very definite about which animals are compatible with each other and which are antagonistic. So find out if you're truly suited to your partner.

RAT + RAT
★ *A successful partnership – especially in business. Great buddies but you're bound to compete!*

RAT + OX
★ *Sexually thrilling but disastrous in marriage. Better as a love affair.*

RAT + TIGER
★ *Expect some dramatic clashes of temperament. Lots of friendship but little true passion.*

Eiaha chipa
PAUL GAUGUIN 1848–1903

RAT + RABBIT
★ *You think Rabbits lack spunk. Conversely, you thrive on adventure. Result? Frustration.*

RAT + DRAGON
★ *A brilliant relationship – plenty of understanding and passion. Star-tipped for happiness.*

RAT + SNAKE
★ *If you work on the differences in your characters, you could learn a great deal from each other.*

RAT + HORSE
★ *No love lost between you two.*

RAT + SHEEP
★ *An uphill struggle at times, though you could make it work with goodwill on both sides.*

RAT + MONKEY
★ *A shared outlook and a common understanding.*

LOVE PARTNERS AT A GLANCE

Rat with:	Tips on Togetherness	Compatibility
Rat	beware rivalry	♥♥♥
Ox	mutual appreciation	♥♥♥
Tiger	learn to compromise	♥♥
Rabbit	on different wave-lengths	♥
Dragon	on cloud nine	♥♥♥♥
Snake	an alluring fascination	♥♥♥
Horse	an unstable union	♥
Sheep	at odds	♥
Monkey	irresistible magnetism	♥♥♥♥
Rooster	too many differences	♥
Dog	mutual respect	♥♥
Pig	great happiness and good friends	♥♥♥

COMPATIBILITY RATINGS:
♥ *conflict* ♥♥ *work at it* ♥♥♥ *strong sexual attraction* ♥♥♥♥ *heavenly!*

RAT + ROOSTER
★ *More scratchy conflict
than there is love.*

RAT + DOG
★ *You find Dogs dull,
but can achieve a stable union.*

RAT + PIG
★ *A roller-coaster
relationship. Terrific
companionship and attraction,
but watch those bills!*

Hot Dates

IF YOU'RE DATING someone for the first time, taking your partner out for a special occasion or simply wanting to re-ignite that flame of passion between you, it helps to understand what would please that person most.

RATS ★ *Wine and dine him or take her to a party. Do something on impulse… go to the races or take a flight in a hot air balloon.*

OXEN ★ *Go for a drive in the country and drop in on a stately home. Visit an art gallery or antique shops. Then have an intimate dinner à deux.*

'So glad to see you…'
COCA-COLA 1945

TIGERS ★ *Tigers thrive on excitement so go clay-pigeon shooting, Formula One racing or challenge each other to a Quasar dual. A date at the theatre will put stars in your Tiger's eyes.*

RABBITS ★ *Gentle and creative, your Rabbit date will enjoy an evening at home with some take-away food and a romantic video. Play some seductive jazz and snuggle up.*

DRAGONS ★ *Mystery and magic will thrill your Dragon date. Take in a son et lumière show or go to a carnival. Or drive to the coast and sink your toes in the sand as the sun sets.*

SNAKES ★ *Don't do anything too active – these creatures like to take life slooooowly. Hire a row-boat for a long, lazy ride down the river. Give a soothing massage, then glide into a sensual jacuzzi together.*

The Carnival
GASTON-DOIN 19/20TH CENTURY

HORSES ★ *Your zany Horse gets easily bored. Take her on a mind-spinning tour of the local attractions. Surprise him with tickets to a musical show. Whatever you do, keep them guessing.*

SHEEP ★ *These folk adore the Arts so visit a museum, gallery or poetry recital. Go to a concert, the ballet, or the opera.*

MONKEYS ★ *The fantastical appeals to this partner, so go to a fancy-dress party or a masked ball, a laser light show or a sci-fi movie.*

ROOSTERS ★ *Grand gestures will impress your Rooster. Escort her to a film première or him to a formal engagement. Dressing up will place this date in seventh heaven.*

DOGS ★ *A cosy, candle-lit dinner will please this most unassuming of partners more than any social occasion. Chatting and story telling will ensure a close understanding.*

PIGS ★ *Arrange a slap-up meal or a lively party, or cruise through the shopping mall. Shopping is one of this partner's favourite hobbies!*

Year of Commitment

CAN THE YEAR in which you marry (or make a firm commitment to live together) have any influence upon your marital relationship or the life you and your partner forge together? According to the Orientals, it certainly can. Whether your marriage is fiery, gentle, productive, passionate, insular or sociable doesn't so much depend on your animal nature, as on the nature of the Animal in whose year you tied the knot.

Detail from Chinese Marriage Ceremony
CHINESE PAINTING

IF YOU MARRY IN A YEAR OF THE...

RAT ★ *your marriage should succeed because ventures starting now attract long-term success. Materially, you won't want and life is full of friendship.*

Marriage Feast
CHINESE PAINTING

OX ★ *your relationship will be solid and tastes conventional. Diligence will be recognized and you'll be well respected.*

TIGER ★ *you'll need plenty of humour to ride out the storms. Marrying in the Year of the Tiger is not auspicious.*

RABBIT ★ *you're wedded under the emblem of lovers. It's auspicious for a happy, carefree relationship, as neither partner wants to rock the boat.*

DRAGON ★ *you're blessed. This year is highly auspicious for luck, happiness and success.*

SNAKE ★ *it's good for romance but sexual entanglements are rife. Your relationship may seem languid, but passions run deep.*

HORSE ★ *chances are you decided to marry on the spur of the moment as the Horse year encourages impetuous behaviour. Marriage now may be volatile.*

SHEEP ★ *your family and home are blessed but watch domestic spending. Money is very easily frittered away.*

Marriage Ceremony
CHINESE PAINTING

MONKEY ★ *married life could be unconventional. As plans go awry your lives could be full of surprises.*

ROOSTER ★ *drama characterizes your married life. Your household will run like clockwork, but bickering could strain your relationship.*

DOG ★ *it's a truly fortunate year and you can expect domestic joy. Prepare for a large family as the Dog is the sign of fertility!*

PIG ★ *it's highly auspicious and there'll be plenty of fun. Watch out for indulgence and excess.*

Marriage Ceremony (detail)

Detail from Chinese Marriage Ceremony
CHINESE PAINTING

鼠

TYPICAL RAT PLEASURES

COLOUR PREFERENCES ★ Light blue

Garnet

Amethyst

Diamond

GEMS AND STONES ★ Diamond, amethyst, garnet

SUITABLE GIFTS ★ Construction kits, art books, maps, food hamper, a subscription to a sports centre, car accessories

Monte Meteora, Greece with Roussanou Monastery
FOUNDED 1388

HOBBIES AND PASTIMES ★ Cricket , basketball, DIY, interior design, handicrafts, painting, collecting

HOLIDAY PREFERENCES ★ Rats like to keep moving so travel is a delight. Lying on a beach is not for you. You'll want to explore, take in the night life, experience all the sights, and experiment with the foreign tastes and smells.

COUNTRIES LINKED WITH THE RAT ★ China, Japan, South Africa, Greece, Turkey, Albania, Bulgaria and the former Yugoslavia

The Rat Parent

Sakyamuni, Confucius and Lao Tzu (detail)
WANG SHU-KU PAINTING

鼠

31

AS A RAT PARENT, you're devoted to your children. You surround them with affection and laugh good-humouredly at all their antics. When they're little you fret a good deal over them. You agonize about whether you're bringing them up correctly. You are able to pick things up in a flash, so you do tend to get impatient with people who aren't quite as quick-witted. This could become a potential source of conflict between you and your offspring, should any of them happen to be late-developers.

INDULGENCE

On the whole, you're a generous parent who can't deny your little ones anything they want – and they soon learn how to twist you around their little fingers.

THE RAT HABITAT

As a Rat, you're a happy home-maker and are always willing to share the household chores. You're not particularly interested in keeping up with the Joneses and it doesn't matter to you whether or not your furnishings are up-to-date. What does matter, though, is your home is warm and comfortable. Light blue is likely to be prominent in your choice of décor. And because yours is the sign of acquisition, your house is probably bursting with all the bits and pieces you've collected over the years. You're a happy, domesticated individual who finds joy in your home and family.

32

Animal Babies

FOR SOME parents, their children's personalities harmonize perfectly with their own. Others find that no matter how much they may love their offspring they're just not on the same wavelength.

Our children arrive with their characters already well formed and, according to Chinese philosophy, shaped by the influence of their Animal Year. So you should be mindful of the year in which you conceive.

BABIES BORN IN THE YEAR OF THE...

RAT ★ *love being cuddled. They keep on the go – so give them plenty of rest. Later they enjoy collecting things.*

OX ★ *are placid, solid and independent. If not left to their own devices they sulk.*

TIGER ★ *are happy and endearing. As children, they have irrepressible energy. Boys are sporty and girls tom-boys.*

RABBIT ★ *are sensitive and strongly bonded to their mother. They need stability to thrive.*

DRAGON ★ *are independent and imaginative from the start. Encourage any interest that will allow their talents to flourish.*

SNAKE ★ *have great charm. They are slow starters so may need help with school work. Teach them to express feelings.*

One Hundred Children Scroll
ANON, MING PERIOD

HORSE ★ *will burble away contentedly for hours. Talking starts early and they excel in languages.*

SHEEP ★ *are placid, well-behaved and respectful. They are family-oriented and never stray too far from home.*

MONKEY ★ *take an insatiable interest in everything. With agile minds they're quick to learn. They're good-humoured but mischievous!*

ROOSTER ★ *are sociable. Bright and vivacious, their strong adventurous streak best shows itself on a sports field.*

DOG ★ *are cute and cuddly. Easily pleased, they are content just pottering around the house amusing themselves for hours. Common sense is their greatest virtue.*

PIG ★ *are affectionate and friendly. Well-balanced, self-confident children, they're happy-go-lucky and laid-back. They are popular with friends.*

Health, Wealth and Worldly Affairs

BECAUSE YOUR SIGN influence is active you have enough stamina to fight any illness that may befall you. As a Rat, you're highly-strung and prone to tension. A tendency to fret aggravates the stress problem. Also, all Rats share an undercurrent of aggression, which they generally manage to keep well under control but which will find a release in active sports. Practising yoga or meditation would also help.

Summer in Peking
WANG DA GUANG 20TH CENTURY

Though you're industrious by nature, routine grinds you down so a job with variety and flexible hours would suit you best. Above all else, you function much better as a boss than you do as an underling.

CAREER

The Chinese say that, as an advisor, the Rat should be listened to. It's well recognized that you possess vision and foresight and can see problems clearly, and are able to take an objective view. You're a shrewd operator and your sixth sense alerts you to opportunities coming your way and warns you of potential problems.

鼠

Delivering Grain to the State
CHOU WEN-TEH PAINTING

FINANCES

Clever and thrifty, you have a gift with money and are compelled to put something aside for a rainy day. You're either a terrific saver or, in lean times, know how to turn something to your advantage. The Chinese have a proverb: *they who pile up grain hoards have much to lose.*

FRIENDSHIPS

Generally cheerful and sociable with a knack for putting people at their ease, it's not surprising that you're popular. You're an interesting conversationalist and there's always that famous Rat allure.

In business, a career you're eminently suited to, you're an honest broker even though you do have an eye on the main chance. Power, position, money and prestige are all-important to you and you have an in-built knack of talking your way through obstacles in order to reach your goals.

RATS MAKE EXCELLENT:

Writers ★ Broadcasters ★ Actors ★ Advisors
Counsellors ★ Lawyers ★ Politicians ★ Designers
Engineers ★ Managers ★ Directors ★ Administrators
Entrepreneurs ★ Musicians ★ Stand-up comedians
Researchers ★ Historians ★ Racing-drivers

36

East Meets West

COMBINE YOUR Oriental Animal sign with your Western Zodiac birth sign to form a deeper and richer understanding of your character and personality.

ARIES RAT
★ *You're active in your work and in love. With typical enthusiasm you can party till dawn and your charm ensures you have no problems getting partners.*

TAUREAN RAT
★ *In matters of the heart, you have your head screwed on. You may give in to your sensuality when young, but what you look for is security. When you find your ideal mate you'll stick to him or her like glue.*

GEMINI RAT
★ *Quick, clever and easily bored, you thrive on variety. Your problem is indecision and to choose one person with whom to settle down is difficult. Having made your choice, the next problem is sticking to it.*

CANCERIAN RAT
★ *Because you're sensitive, you hide your feelings and this can make you unfathomable. Material comforts are important but far more critical is a close-knit family. You make an intuitive and understanding lover.*

LEONINE RAT
★ *You are a charismatic figure, dynamic, generous and responsive, which guarantees you worldly and romantic success. When you fall in love, it's totally and you ask to be loved utterly in return.*

VIRGO RAT
★ *Your mission is to love and serve but your charming naivety can attract lame ducks. You care desperately about other people but beware that they don't take advantage of you.*

LIBRAN RAT
★ *Elegant and refined, you live a cultured life-style. You're charming and sophisticated and you're in love with love. Your ideal partner must be sweet-natured and tender because coarseness and bad manners of any sort upset you deeply. Moreover, he or she must possess drop-dead good looks.*

SCORPIO RAT
★ *Being born a Scorpio Rat means you're driven by your emotions. Passionate and intense, you smoulder with desire, you're incandescent with jealousy, you burn with revenge. For you, love is never to be trifled with.*

SAGITTARIAN RAT
★ *With restlessness in your soul, the last thing you want is to settle down in a cosy, suburban existence. Lady Luck constantly smiles on you but true love may be elusive as you fear that commitment will mean losing the independence that you hold so dear.*

CAPRICORN RAT
★ *For you, life is a serious business. You may not be the most romantic or sentimental of Rats, but you're practical and level-headed and you look for a partner with the same virtues as yourself. In marriage you're as faithful and true as the live-long day.*

AQUARIAN RAT
★ *Original and individualistic, you take a liberal attitude to most things. By other people's standards, you may be unconventional. As long as you have plenty of friends and an intellectual rapport with your partner, who cares about the neighbours.*

PISCEAN RAT
★ *Even though you're highly artistic and creatively talented, you lack self-confidence in your own abilities. You function better as part of a team than you do on your own. A close, loving and supportive relationship is central to your happiness.*

鼠

38

FAMOUS RATS

Andrew Lloyd
Webber

Doris Day

The Duke of York

Shakespeare

Yves St Laurent

Claude Monet

Charlotte Brontë

Mati Hari

Galileo

Monet ⋆ Charlotte Brontë ⋆ Lord Louis Mountbatten
Shakespeare ⋆ Tennessee Williams ⋆ Galileo
HM Queen Elizabeth the Queen Mother
FW Woolworth ⋆ Prince Harry
Marlon Brando ⋆ Charles, Prince of Wales
The Duke of York ⋆ Wayne Sleep
Yves St Laurent ⋆ Mata Hari ⋆ Doris Day
Andrew Lloyd Webber ⋆ Glenda Jackson

Charles,
Prince of Wales

The Rat Year in Focus

SINCE EVERY YEAR of the Rat opens a new cycle, this is an excellent 12-month period for fresh starts. Launch new products, get married, buy a house, start a family or turn over a new leaf now.

SLOW BUT SURE

In Rat Years, market economies are buoyant and spirits rise. But don't expect ventures to yield quick returns. This is not in the nature of the Rat, whose influence favours the careful investor. Many, who have bet the shirts off their backs in a Rat Year, have lost them.

Dreaming of Immortality in a Thatched Cottage (detail) T'ANG YIN MING DYNASTY

NO TIME FOR COMPLACENCY

Remember the Rat is constantly on the go, using his wits, with his eye always on the main chance. Opportunities will abound and the quick and the smart will turn them to their own advantage.

ACTIVITIES ASSOCIATED WITH THE RAT YEAR

The discovery, invention, patenting, marketing or manufacturing of: the transistor, CS gas, self-winding watch, stainless steel, communication satellites, lasers, contraception and long-playing records.

THE
RAT

40

Your Rat Fortunes
for the Next 12 Years

1996 MARKS THE BEGINNING of a new 12-year cycle in the Chinese calendar. How your relationships and worldly prospects fare will depend on the influence of each Animal year in turn.

1996 YEAR OF THE RAT — *19 Feb 1996 – 6 Feb 1997*

This is a busy year for you and one which augurs well for your worldly aspirations. Career-wise you could be taking a leap forward. There'll be new opportunities financially and socially. New friendships could blossom into long-term romance.

YEAR TREND: PROGRESSIVE

1997 YEAR OF THE OX — *7 Feb 1997 – 27 Jan 1998*

Following last year's career advancement, you now begin to feel

the pressure. But you should make steady progress in 1997. No major domestic upheavals are forecast and family life is a source of joy.

YEAR TREND: STABLE

1998 YEAR OF THE TIGER — *28 Jan 1998 – 15 Feb 1999*

Rats are famous for their rashness. As 1998 carries elements that are unpredictable, you are advised to avoid taking unwise risks. Travel could figure strongly. For some, this year may herald the parting of the ways.

YEAR TREND: FAIR

1999 YEAR OF THE RABBIT | *16 Feb 1999 – 4 Feb 2000*

The slower pace of the Rabbit years is not suited to your ambitious mentality so you may be champing at the bit in 1999. Relax, let your hair down, and spend quality time with your family.

YEAR TREND: FRUSTRATING

2000 YEAR OF THE DRAGON | *5 Feb 2000 – 23 Jan 2001*

This is more your kind of year: pacy, daring and exciting – a year of lucky breaks and lucky escapes. Your career prospects are exceedingly good, finances are buoyant and love affairs exciting. But do not to allow others to exploit your generosity.

YEAR TREND: HIGHLY SUCCESSFUL

The Chinese calendar runs in 12-year cycles.

2001 YEAR OF THE SNAKE | *24 Jan 2001 – 11 Feb 2002*

Things are never what they seem in a Year of the Snake. So read the small print and study people's body language carefully. If you don't, you could be out of pocket or bruised – physically and emotionally. Prospects improve at the end of the year.

YEAR TREND: APPROACH WITH CAUTION

42

2002 YEAR OF THE HORSE *12 Feb 2002 – 31 Jan 2003*

The impulsive elements of the Year of the Horse
will exacerbate your already rash tendencies. You'll
be tempted to spend more than you can afford;
relationships could become messy.

YEAR TREND: VOLATILE

2003 YEAR OF THE SHEEP *1 Feb 2003 – 21 Jan 2004*

After the turmoil of the last year, in the Year of
the Sheep you can regain lost ground. There'll be
opportunities to sort out your finances, and career
and occupation take on a renewed impetus.
Relations with loved ones can be mended.

YEAR TREND: IMPROVEMENT AND RECOVERY

2004 YEAR OF THE MONKEY *22 Jan 2004 – 8 Feb 2005*

The inventive jollity of the Monkey influence is
conducive to your sense of adventure. This year
your fertile mind can pay dividends. Your social
life will be buoyant, domestic affairs should be
harmonious and romance brings a lightness of heart.

YEAR TREND: A TIME FOR ENJOYMENT

*Wind-blown Waves
at Shichi-ri (detail)*
HIROSHIGE

Social life will be buoyant.

2005 YEAR OF THE ROOSTER | 9 Feb 2005 – 28 Jan 2006

Events happen thick and fast in this Rooster Year, keeping you active. What appear to be obstacles or challenges will turn out to be blessings in disguise. Disagreements between existing partners can begin to be resolved and those seeking romance could find it this year.

YEAR TREND: SET-BACKS BUT POSITIVE SURPRISES

2006 YEAR OF THE DOG | 29 Jan 2006 – 17 Feb 2007

This year you could take on more than you can deal with. There'll be people who'll reach out to help, but don't take them for granted. It is not a good year for relationships

YEAR TREND: UNSETTLING

2007 YEAR OF THE PIG | 18 Feb 2007 – 6 Feb 2008

Relationships should start to improve. Understanding between you and your partner returns. If you've gone your separate ways, this is the year to make a fresh start. Socially, the tempo will increase, with opportunities to link up with the person of your dreams.

YEAR TREND: PREPARATION FOR THE NEW

PICTURE CREDITS

AKG Berlin/Erich Lessing: p.24L
AKG London: pp.21, 24B, 25R
e. t. archive: pp.9, 25T, 30, 34; British Museum: 31,
    33T; Freer Gallery of Art: 39; Private Collection: 26,
    27B; Victoria & Albert Museum: 28, 29, 42
Fine Art Photographic Library Ltd: pp.27T, 32-3
Hulton Deutsch Collection: p.38 (all except Doris Day)
Images Colour Library: pp.8, 22T & B, 23
Kobal Collection: p.38 (Doris Day)